DRAG BIKES

MOTORCYCLE MANIA

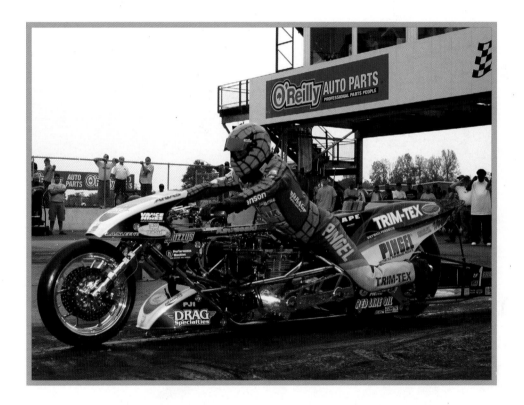

David and Patricia Armentrout

Rourke
Publishing LLC
Vero Beach, Florida 32964

www.rourkepublishing.com

PHOTO CREDITS: All images ©Matt Polito/racingperspectives.com

Title page: *A drag racer straddles his powerful machine.*

Editor: Frank Sloan

Cover and page design by Nicola Stratford

Library of Congress Cataloging-in-Publication Data

Armentrout, David, 1962-
 Drag bikes / David and Patricia Armentrout.
     p. cm. -- (Motorcycle mania)
 Includes bibliographical references and index.
 ISBN 1-59515-454-X (hardcover)
 1. Drag bikes--Juvenile literature. I. Armentrout, Patricia, 1960- II.
Title. III. Series.

  TL442.5.A76 2006
  629.227'5--dc22

2005010709

Printed in the USA

CG/CG

Rourke Publishing
1-800-394-7055
www.rourkepublishing.com
sales@rourkepublishing.com
Post Office Box 3328, Vero Beach, FL 32964

TABLE OF CONTENTS

There's Nothing Like a Drag Race 4

Racing by the Rules 8

Racing Classes 10

Odd-looking Machines...........................14

Ready to Race 16

Who Wins? 19

Top Fuel Dragsters 21

Glossary 23

Index 24

Further Reading/Websites to Visit........24

THERE'S NOTHING LIKE A DRAG RACE

Drag bike racing is like no other racing sport. It pits two riders and their bikes in straight-line racing. Of course, not every motorbike rider can handle a drag bike, and not every rider wants to. But, for riders who love competition, speed, and the smell of nitro in the air, there's nothing like a drag race!

Nitro is short for **nitromethane**—the fuel used to run the engines of top fuel dragsters.

Fans witness the final round of a pro-class Harley event.

A drag race is an **acceleration** contest between two vehicles over a measured distance, usually a quarter-mile (1,320 feet/402.3 meters) or an eighth-mile (660 feet/201.2 meters). A drag race takes place on a drag strip—a pair of straight lanes.

Racers lean forward and hold on tight as they cruise down the strip.

Drag bikes don't turn easily, so racers get help backing bikes into position.

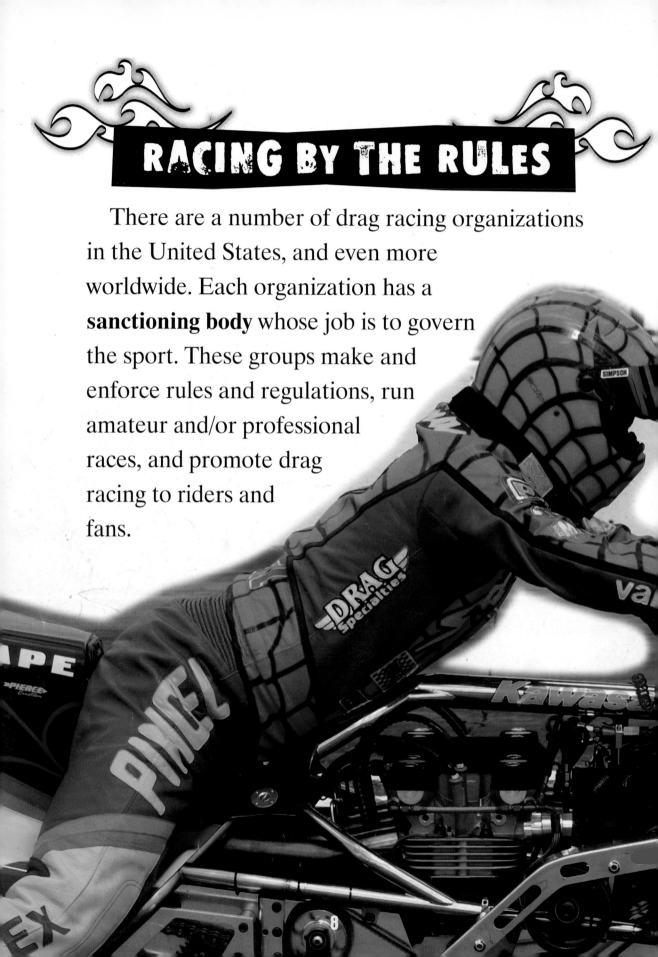

RACING BY THE RULES

There are a number of drag racing organizations in the United States, and even more worldwide. Each organization has a **sanctioning body** whose job is to govern the sport. These groups make and enforce rules and regulations, run amateur and/or professional races, and promote drag racing to riders and fans.

An organization's long list of rules and regulations include bike safety requirements and inspections, helmet and clothing requirements for the riders and crew, and race procedures.

RACING CLASSES

Because bikes differ, racers are placed in a category that fits their bike's classification. A racer may qualify for a number of races, depending on the bike (sport bike, Harley, modified stock bike, etc.), engine size, tire size, fuel type, and so on.

A sportsman class dragster competes in a super eliminator race.

The All Harley Drag Racing Association (AHDRA), for instance, has several racing classes: Super Sport, Pro Stock, and Top Fuel are just a few. The Texas Shootout Motorcycle Drag Racing Sanction lists eight classes. One class, called Street E.T., allows street legal bikes to race and is geared toward the beginner drag racer.

E.T. stands for elapsed time—the time it takes a bike to travel from the starting line to the finish line. Elapsed time helps measure performance and is sometimes used to determine a **handicap**.

New riders typically start their careers racing in a street bike category.

ODD-LOOKING MACHINES

Bikes designed specifically for drag racing look odd. The front tires are small. The rear tires, called "slicks," are big and smooth. Some drag bikes have a wheelie bar—two tiny wheels attached to a long strut in the rear.

Drivers look uncomfortable straddling their machines. They lean forward across the bike grasping the handlebars. This position helps keep the rider on the bike as he or she accelerates, and it's more **aerodynamic**.

A wheelie bar prevents a wheelie. A wheelie is when the front tire lifts off the ground during a hard and fast acceleration.

Wheelie bars in the rear keep the front wheel from coming too far off the ground.

Before the race a rider will perform a **burnout**. This is when he or she spins the rear tire in water to heat and clean it. The tire gets hot and sticky so it gets better traction. Burnouts produce a thick cloud of smoke that only adds to the excitement and atmosphere of a racing event.

A hot, sticky back tire improves traction.

A racer rolls his bike toward the staging beam while keeping an eye on the tree of lights.

Long gone are the days when a drag strip official started a race with the lowering of a flag. This fast-paced motorsport now uses an electronic starting system.

Riders know when to begin a race by watching a tower of colored lights called a Christmas tree. Racers use the tree as their visual countdown. As racers approach the starting line, their front wheels trigger the pre-stage lights to turn on. A second row of lights glows when the front wheels interrupt a light beam that stretches across both lanes. When the racers see green they are free to take off from the starting line. This automatically activates a timer which stops when the riders cross the finish line. Because reaction time makes all the difference, the majority of drag races are won or lost at the starting line.

WHO WINS?

Drag bikes are all about racing, and racing is all about winning. The object is to make it to the finish line in less time than your opponent. If you lose, you are eliminated. If you win, you move on to the next round. When one rider remains, that person is declared the winner of the race category.

A dragster moves on to the final round of a Harley pro-modified class race.

A sportbike racing team poses in the winner's circle.

TOP FUEL DRAGSTERS

Top fuel dragsters are the fastest drag bikes around. These bikes run on an expensive fuel called nitromethane. Some riders competing in this category cross the finish line in under seven seconds, reaching speeds of over 200 miles (321.87 kilometers) an hour!

Some U.S. drag bike organizations:

AHDRA
All Harley Drag Racing Association

NMRA
National Motorcycle Racing Association

PMRA
Professional Motorcycle Racing Association

AMA/PROSTAR
American Motorcycle Association ProStar

AMRA
American Motorcycle Association-all Harleys

Texas Shootout Motorcycle Drag Racing Sanction

Wild and colorful bike designs reflect the personality of racers.

GLOSSARY

acceleration (ak SEL uh RAY shun) — speeding up, going faster and faster

aerodynamic (AIR oh dye NAM ik) — designed to move through the air easily and quickly

burnout (BURN OUT) — spinning the rear tire to heat it prior to every run for better traction

handicap (HAN dee KAP) — in drag bike racing, when a slower motorcycle gets a head start equal to the difference of the two bikes racing

nitromethane (NI tro METH AYN) — the fuel used to run top fuel dragsters

sanctioning body (SANGK shun ing BOD ee) — a group of people who set and enforce laws, rules, and guidelines for a larger organization

INDEX

burnout   16

categories   10, 19, 21

Christmas tree   18

classes   10, 12

drag strip   6, 17

nitro   4, 21

racing organizations   8, 9, 12, 21

regulations   8, 9

rules   8, 9

top-fuel dragsters   4, 21

FURTHER READING

Gibbs, Lynne. *Mega Book of Motorcycles*. Chrysalis Education, 2003.

Hill, Lee Sullivan. *Motorcycles*. Lerner, 2004

Murphy, Tom. *When the Light Turns Green: A Handbook of Motorcycle Drag Racing*. Whitehorse Press, 2002

WEBSITES TO VISIT

All Harley Drag Racing Association
    www.ahdra.com/
PROSTAR Motorcycle Drag Racing
    www.amaprostar.com/
Dragbike Magazine—An on-line magazine that covers all aspects of motorcycle drag racing
    www.dragbike.com/

ABOUT THE AUTHORS

David and Patricia Armentrout specialize in writing nonfiction books for young readers. They have had several books published for primary school reading. The Armentrouts live in Cincinnati, Ohio, with their two children.